Not My Mother's 60

A Baby Boomer's Wisdom On Life's Journey Toward Super Adulthood

Paula Preston Hultman

DEDICATION

To my husband, George; my children, Scott and Alison; and
my extraordinary family and friends. Thank you for your
encouragement, support, and unconditional love.

Acknowledgments

My journey to 60 was never a lonely one, and without my village of family and friends, my life would be meaningless. I want to extend my heartfelt gratitude to everyone who is mentioned in these pages. A special thank you to Deena, my mentor, for being the force that awakened my previously stalled momentum. I am forever grateful for your guidance.

You are all loved more than you will ever know.

INTRODUCTION

I entered the world in the middle—the middle of the century, the middle of the baby boom, to a marvelously middle-class family. Life has been a wonderful adventure with my husband of 42 years. Our two grown children have begun their own journeys, and our family and friends enrich the fabric of our lives. Life has been beautiful. Yet something strange happened on my 59th birthday. It began as a soft murmur and slowly gained volume until it became a deafening internal roar—"YOU ARE GOING TO BE 60!" How the hell did that happen?

As much as I had been in quiet denial about this reality, I was powerless over the fact—60 Happens!

Instead of bemoaning my fate, I decided to celebrate this milestone by writing a blog—*Not My Mother's 60*. It became my therapy of sorts. Step one on my road to acceptance of my upcoming birthday. And I discovered that my observations and wisdom were meaningful to others besides myself! I was encouraged to create a book with my blog posts—and this is the result.

My "30 Toward 60" blog was written in the days approaching my Big 6-0, as a daily dose of 3-Word Wisdom. While not all may strike a chord with you, I hope in these pages you find a bit of helpful wisdom as you follow your path—your journey through each decade.

Please join me as I share my "mid-century modern" observations.

1. Look Out 60!

The countdown began. My 60th birthday was around the corner. How did this happen? Why was I having such a hard time with this number? For someone who absolutely loves the attention bestowed upon her on the anniversary of each trip around the sun, this was the first and only birthday that I had ever dreaded.

At 30, I was a working mother with an infant daughter and energetic toddler son. I had no time to celebrate that birthday, but it became a historic date with John Hinckley's failed assassination of President Ronald Reagan. My husband and I celebrated our 40th birthdays together, with a huge party that cost more than our wedding reception. No black "Over the Hill" balloons for us—40 was fabulous! Even 50 was a birthday I welcomed, commencing with an entire weekend of girly fun with 20 dear friends and family in Palm Springs—secretly planned and precisely executed by my then-20-something daughter and beautiful nieces. Now, 60 was looming—and it was a milestone I not only dreaded but also refused to verbally acknowledge. Why was turning 60 so hard to accept?

Before I go further, let me share a little bit about my super adult self…in no particular order. I am active. I am healthy. I eat right and take my vitamins. I have been a teacher, a business owner, and was recognized as a pillar of our community for my entrepreneurial accomplishments. I currently work in the world of fundraising event production with nonprofits.

I have too many pairs of shoes. I can no longer read without glasses, and I have almost as many pairs of readers as I have footwear. I love to dance. I cherish friendships. I am the queen of entertaining. I say the F-word occasionally. I enjoy my kids' friends—and they like me. I drive faster than I should. I have officiated two weddings. I have had no "work" done—and I have the wrinkles to prove it. I know all of the words to "Bohemian Rhapsody," "Piano Man," and "Me and Bobby McGee," to name just a few—and I sing along loudly every time I hear these and other classics. I cry at weddings and Hallmark commercials. I am a bleeding-heart liberal. I am tolerant. I am not tolerant of intolerance. I love my husband, my kids, and their spouses. I adore my children and the grandchildren they have rewarded me with. I have a wonderful life.

During my aforementioned meltdown, I found myself in a dark place that can only be understood by those facing the reality they have lived more years of their natural life than they have remaining. Proverbially upbeat Paula slipped into a depression of sorts—a nearly suffocating, all-consuming onslaught of negativity, fear, and remorse. We aren't prepared for retirement. This house is too big for us. I am not where I thought I would be in my career. It's too late to start over. Why didn't I write my book? What have I done with my 60 years? I found myself in such a dangerous state of mind that it scared the crap out of me. And the angst was all due to a stupid numeral. I was giving 60 too much negative power.

Thankfully my husband is a great listener and my best friend, and after I confided in him my innermost fears, he gave me what

I needed at that moment—his unconditional love and support. He heard me. He understood. He reminded me we are in this together and helped me get through my lowest of moments. It was time to start doing something. I have so much to be grateful for, and I refuse to be defined by a birth date.

Hello, world—my name is Paula, and I am 60. Another year closer to being a super adult (a friend reported the use of this reference on a fare schedule in Scotland, and I'm adopting it… So much better than *senior citizen*). I will celebrate by sharing my 60 years of life experience and wisdom. I will show the world what the new 60 looks like. My 60 will not be my mother's 60. My 60 will be a new and improved 60.

Today's 3-Word Wisdom Look Out 60— while the number is daunting, it's also inevitable. Ready or not, Paula's on her way!

2. FIND YOUR SOULMATE

Try as one might, there is no defying the effects of gravity on the aging process. Sure, you can spend your children's inheritance on any variety of "procedures" to be plumped, tucked, and altered into an often-unrecognizable version of your former self. In my case, there is no inheritance to spend! But even if I could, I am not sure I would take drastic measures to regain my youthful glow—or would I? For now, I have my fountain of youth—my husband—who still makes me feel as if I am the most beautiful woman in the world, every single day.

Have I mentioned that I love my husband? He and I met in high school in 1968—Senior English, to be exact—when he was into muscle cars and I was into folk music, college boys, and the peace movement. We did not have a lot in common in those days, and I'm sure he had no idea who I was at first. But I knew him—he was POPULAR! When I walked into the already seated classroom and passed by his desk to give my transfer papers to the teacher, he noticed ME! Bookish, shy, want-to-be-in-the-background Paula. The very next day, his desk was next to mine—he had a way with teachers and managed to convince her he needed to be at the front of the room in order to see better! From that high school "senior" moment we were friends. We attended senior class functions together as friends. We counseled each other through different relationships and headed off to different colleges. It wasn't until two years later, with only occasional contact in the interim, that we realized our friendship had blossomed into something more. I could go on about our story, but I'll cut to the chase—we met in 1968, started dating in 1971 and fell in love, got engaged in 1972, and married in 1974. And we have been beside each other—for better and for worse—ever since.

We are both turning 60 this year. In fact, for six weeks he will be in his 60s, and I will still be in my 50s. I always use these weeks to remind him that I am younger than him! For him, this is simply another birthday. No drama, no angst. Just a birthday with the obligatory cards, a gift or two (his gifts of choice—socks and ties...really?), his favorite dinner and dessert, and a nice gathering of family and friends. Over. Done. Move on. He deserves some attention for his 60-year milestone, yet he has had to take on all of my anxiety and is watching over me as if I am a delicate Fabergé egg—handling me with care as I attempt to wrap my head around our entry into senior citizenship. If there were an Oscar for Outstanding Achievement in the Husband Role, he would be a recipient.

I deal with the physical reminders of aging every time I glance into my 8X magnifying mirror (ugh). I see almost-60 Paula. He, on the other hand, sees me through a different lens. In his eyes, I am still 17-year-old Paula who walked into English class and caught his attention. A day doesn't go by that I don't get some sort of acknowledgment I am beautiful in his eyes. I don't want to give TMI here (my kids read this!), but my husband still thinks I'm hot!

It's becoming clear to me that one of the biggest advantages of knowing someone for 42 years is the magic of their internal lens—our mind's eye imprints the original "photograph" of that first encounter indelibly and forever. To each other, we are still crazy kids in love. We see past the gray hair (his, not mine—thanks to my stylist and her magic potions), the age spots (can't I still call them freckles?), and the oh-so-unattractive arm wattle! Turning 60 with my best friend is the only gift I need to mark this momentous occasion. Well, that…and maybe a Fabergé egg!

Today's 3-Word Wisdom – Find Your Soulmate. There's nothing better than sharing life's adventures with the person who fills your heart with joy.

3. SAVOR LIFE'S MEMORIES

Be prepared, folks. As you approach 60, you will need a reliable memory back-up system to keep yourself on track. I used to rely on a lovely week-at-a-glance yearly planner from the Metropolitan Museum of Art. Its only drawback was its static placement in my kitchen "command center." Being a tech-savvy super adult, I now keep track of life's events on my computer's Outlook calendar, which syncs with my iPhone. This calendar, complete with its thoughtful little reminders that pop up 15 minutes before every scheduled event or task, is my personal assistant and social secretary. Every appointment, meeting, weekly work schedule, birthday, and weekend activity resides in the memory of my Outlook calendar. My back-up to the back-up system is an assortment of memo pads and Post-it notes, as well as an occasional empty food wrapper on the kitchen counter reminding me to add that item to my grocery list. Don't laugh. It works for me, and I can proudly say I am on time for (most) appointments, I send birthday greetings on the correct date, and I show up at baby and bridal showers on time. That is, unless my computer and 4G network fail me.

One thing I need no help remembering is nearly every detail of my childhood. Those recollections are etched in my memory as clearly as if they occurred yesterday! For those of you who are on this baby boomer journey with me, let's take a trip down memory lane... Who remembers these bits of '50s and '60s pop culture and history?

- *The Ed Sullivan Show* (name your three favorite guests)
- Skate keys (on a shoestring around your neck, to tighten your skates to your saddle shoes)
- Hula-Hoops (one of my 15 seconds of fame was introducing the first Hula-Hoop to rural South Dakota kids when I was eight years old—I was one cool Southern California kid)
- Petticoats with layers and layers of crinkly crinoline, worn under your school dresses (no pants allowed for girls)
- Toni permanents (I am "cursed" with naturally curly hair and longed for stick-straight tresses, so I was always perplexed by girls who wanted permanents)
- Black-and-white televisions—and your very first color TV
- The arrival of the Beatles to the United States
- The Cuban missile crisis
- Duck-and-cover drills—apparently in the '50s you were safe from the effects of a nuclear blast by simply covering your head and cowering under your desk. Seriously, this was the biggest fear of my childhood. I always wished we had a bomb shelter.
- Where you were when you heard President Kennedy had been assassinated
- Nightly news reports on the casualties of the Vietnam War
- Neil Armstrong's walk on the moon

So many reminiscences…so little time. Suffice it to say that my long-term memory is extraordinary—those slacker short-term memory brain cells could take a lesson from their almost 60-year-old counterparts. Ask me about the '50s and '60s, and I will sing theme songs, pinpoint my exact location when witnessing history, and recall days and dates with impressive accuracy. Ask me to find the everyday tablecloth I tucked away last month for safekeeping over the holidays, and all bets are off.

I have to admit I really, really cherish my childhood memories—along with the recollections of young love, first kisses, our first home, and new babies (yes, even those sleepless nights rocking and walking them for comfort). Super adulthood brings with it a memory cache chock-full of recollections of history and trivia—all of which have played their part in shaping our lives. As I approach 60, I am thankful for all of these memories and want to thank everyone in advance for indulging me in sharing them. Give me long-term memory over short-term any day. If I ask you a question that you recently answered, be kind. Skip the, "Don't you remember…?" lead-in. Simply tell me again. And if I wax nostalgic with the same story more than once—please listen, nod, and chuckle at the content as if you are hearing it for the first time. I must have forgotten I shared it with you just LAST WEEK!

Today's 3-Word Wisdom – Savor Life's Memories. The experiences from your past helped shape your journey. Find joy in the good, forgive the bad, and embrace the history of your past.

4. CHERISH YOUR PENGUINS

It began with a Christmas gift from one friend to three others about 15 years ago. Matching pins—each one a sterling silver penguin with abalone inlay. This was a step up from our usual gift exchange of decorative lemon zesters and scented candles, and it begged the question—did I miss the memo about the increased gift price limit? I wasn't alone in my surprise. Three of the four of us were feeling a bit guilty about our presents soon to be opened—cute cocktail napkins, festive cheese spreaders, and gingerbread man coffee mugs! Our friend had some explaining to do, but first, she had one more gift to bestow—in a red silk pouch. The last gift was another pin—this one a group of penguins—in stunning black coral and mother-of-pearl. With this pin came the story that has bonded us for years and has seen us through the most challenging moments of our lives.

Why penguins? Our friend had done her research. In emperor penguin society, huddling is a survival method. In the frigid arctic winters, penguins form tight groups to protect each other and to conserve body heat. The penguins constantly maneuver themselves from the outside to the inside of the huddle in order for each to have the warmth and protection necessary to conserve energy and avoid starvation or death. The individual penguin pins would become beautiful additions to our personal jewelry collections, but the three-penguin pin would belong to all of us—its next keeper to be determined by whoever currently had the pin in her possession. In our friendship foursome, The Penguin Pin would be symbolic of our "huddle"—if you received it, you knew that, whatever challenge you were facing, your penguins were with you, in a huddle, keeping you warm and safe and loved.

I have a particular fondness for my penguin pals, because in this circle I am the baby penguin—P4—and P1, P2, and P3 are going out of their way to welcome me into their decade! Our huddle has protected every one of us at some time over the years since P1's original gift was shared. There is no meeting of the minds or timeline to determine when and to whom The Pin should be passed. We penguins know when someone is in need of being in the center of the huddle, and over the years, The Pin has been with each one of us when we needed it the most. The Pin spent the better part of 2010 with P3—huddling with her as she fought her battle with breast cancer. The Pin saw her through lumpectomies, mastectomies, and chemo. If one of the penguins was not physically with P3 during her battle, our symbolic huddle never left her side.

There are also times when The Pin celebrates some of the best penguin moments. When P2 and her husband celebrated their 40th anniversary with a renewal of their wedding vows, we offered to be her bridesmaids (as the baby penguin, I volunteered to be the flower girl). After lots of wine and laughter, we assured P2 we would opt for a less-obvious inclusion in the ceremony and presented her with The Pin. We pinned it to her bouquet and "walked" down the aisle with her. It is one of my favorite penguin memories.

In January, after my first blog post admitting my struggles with turning 60, my penguins and I huddled over more wine—another method we use to keep warm—and I confided some of my fears, my regrets, and my lowest moments that had taken me to that dark place I mentioned in my earlier post. I realized I had felt like the penguin on the outer fringe of the huddle, shivering in the cold, fearing my future. Thankfully I had shaken off the negativity and was ready to embrace 60—which, they reminded me, was not a death sentence! Not long afterward, I found the unmistakable red silk pouch on my dresser. There it was. The Pin. P3 was on her way to recovery, and she had quietly passed the huddle to P4—the penguins had my back.

Today's 3-Word Wisdom—Cherish Your Penguins. One benefit of super adulthood is the wealth of memories you can savor—experiences shared with the most important people in your life. My circle of extraordinary friends and family extends beyond The Penguins, and I cannot imagine this journey that has been my life without them sharing it with me. To those of you who haven't already done so, celebrate the penguins in your life. Keep them close, treasure them, and be there when they need warmth, love, and support. Thank you family, friends, and my penguins—you are a magnificent huddle!

5. Forget If-Onlys

As "The Birthday" lurks, I find myself doing a lot of self-reflection—sometimes healthy, occasionally depressing, and at times, embarrassingly trivial—am I too old to shop at a store called Forever 21? Is the expensive night cream really taking years off as promised, or is my presbyopic eyesight simply—and thankfully—blurring the wrinkles? Occasionally I come down with a serious case of the if-onlys—if only I had stayed in the teaching profession until retirement…if only I had applied sunblock every day of my life…if only I had actually used my gym membership! Hey, life, can I get a do-over?

Today's 3-Word Wisdom—Forget If-Onlys. My birthday present to me is a beautifully wrapped gift of self-acceptance. I forgive myself for what I did not accomplish before 60. The choices I made and the paths I took have all contributed to my 60-year adventure. For better or worse, this is Paula, letting go of the shoulda-woulda-coulda's!

6. Write A Letter

We hosted a family reunion a few years ago. For most of those attending, it had been nearly 40 years since we had seen each other, and for many, it was their first introduction to our extended family. It was a glorious weekend of reacquainting and reminiscing.

Of particular interest was the assortment of letters, dating as far back as the 1920s, penned in our late relative's elegant cursive, lovingly signed, dutifully mailed, and gratefully saved. Throughout the weekend, everyone took some time to read the letters—my grandfather's letter to my aunt, sharing the tragic news of my uncle's death on the beaches of Normandy in 1944. Another aunt offering the details of her beautiful daughter's first steps. My then-10-year-old uncle writing a letter to his parents in South Dakota, letting them know that all was well in Canada— his "foster" home with an aunt—during a brutal flu epidemic. On these brittle and yellowed pages were the family history and special moments that carried our ancestors through the best and the worst of times. This wasn't a history book—it was our family experiencing everyday life in historic times. Powerful. Touching. Funny. Real.

As she read her ancestors' personal histories, one of my tween great-nieces commented that she would never have anything like this to share with her offspring. In that moment, the reality of her e-mailed, texted, Facebooked, and Snapchatted world set in. Cyberspace had efficiently delivered her news, yet there was no record of it—simply a delete button.

I will admit my collection of family letters and photos needs some TLC. When I retire, I am determined to organize the contents of the boxes that clutter my closets. Perhaps the same great-niece who was so fascinated with their contents will bring them into the 21st century by scanning them into some sort of family e-book! Don't get me wrong—I am all for progress. I embrace the ease with which we can stay electronically connected—yet I also cherish the memories that reading a piece of handwritten communication can evoke.

Today's 3-Word Wisdom—Write a Letter. Buy some beautiful stationery, and send a handwritten letter to someone special. Take your time. Express yourself thoughtfully and make an effort to show the recipient how much you care. Check your spelling the old-fashioned way—with a dictionary. Address your envelope with love and care. Affix a stamp and find yourself a mailbox. Keep in mind you will not receive the immediate gratification of an instant reply, but enjoy the satisfaction of knowing what your written words may mean to their recipient. Don't let the art of letter writing be lost on the next generation.

7. NURTURE LOVING RELATIONSHIPS

It is no secret I am completely and hopelessly in love with my husband. We are both keenly aware we are blessed to have found our lifelong partners so early in our lives.

"What is the secret to your success?" I get this question from time to time, usually from young people who are still seeking "the one"—or from couples who are new to the adventure, who seem to be in awe that Hubby and I are still so happy together after so many years! Such queries have led me to ask myself what has contributed to our marital longevity. Here is our "recipe:"

- **We nurture both our passion and our friendship.** Hubby and I spent the first two-and-a-half years of our relationship as friends. Our love for each other blossomed as our friendship deepened. He is my very best friend—and the one who still makes my heart flutter.
- **We laugh—a lot!** Nothing breaks the tension of a serious moment or a temporary him vs. her standoff better than the ability to laugh at the situation.
- **We compromise.** One plus one quite often equals two— opinions, solutions, perspectives. We recognize the give and take of our marriage, and we always try to find a mutually acceptable middle ground.

- **We trust each other**—and make sure we are worthy of that trust.
- **We communicate.** This requires the ability to express our feelings—the good, the bad, and the ugly—without making accusations. It is not always perfect, yet we both believe in our relationship strongly enough to engage in the sometimes difficult conversations.
- **We celebrate each other's triumphs** and offer comfort and compassion when they are needed.

No marriage is trouble-free, and I have to admit our wedded bliss has been interrupted by occasional wedded blizzards. During these stormy times, it feels as if our marriage engine is not running on all cylinders. Something is off. Communication is stilted. Our relationship feels mechanical. It's just not fun. Yet during these temporary breakdowns in our ability to connect, the love between us is unwavering. We value our partnership enough to invest in the hard work necessary to weather the occasional marital storm. Remarkably, we have hit only a few potholes along the way—and our relationship has always grown stronger in the aftermath.

Today's 3-Word Wisdom—Nurture Loving Relationships. When you find your true love, be willing to do the work. Savor the bliss and be prepared for an occasional blizzard. Trust, communicate, compromise, celebrate, comfort, laugh, and enjoy the journey with your lover—your best friend.

8. DEFY YOUR GRAVITY

If you love Broadway musicals as much as I do, you may know the origin of this phrase. It is the defining moment in the musical *Wicked*. In the Tony Award–winning performance, Elphaba recognizes she has a power within, and that no one—not even the Wizard—is going to bring her down. I get goose bumps every time I hear that number!

I had to giggle when I applied today's wisdom literally—staring into the mirror at the effects of gravity on my almost-60 body. I'll admit I am self-absorbed enough to long for a wizard to work his magic and somehow levitate certain "parts" to their earlier positions! For now, I am defying this gravity in true Wizard of Oz fashion—with smoke and mirrors (aka Spanx and Wonderbras)!

Today's 3-Word Wisdom—Defy Your Gravity. I am feeling the weight of disappointment right now. I have experienced some personal defeats lately I am trying to overcome. Thankfully, Hubby and children are here for me. The Penguins understand. I have to find a way to defy the gravity that has been pulling me down. And like Elphaba, I am going to fly! Where are my green paint and broomstick?

9. Celebrate Your Children

Hubby and I always knew we wanted to have children. As eager as we were to start our family—he was in law school, and my teaching career was just beginning—parenthood was placed on the back burner. Yet we did find ways to get our kid fix. We frequently borrowed our siblings' kids and enjoyed the easy part of parenting. Aunt Paula and Uncle Hubby were fun to visit. Trips to Disneyland, the zoo, and SeaWorld with happy little rent-a-children on their best behavior—and returnable to their parents before any end-of-day meltdowns. How difficult could parenthood be? We were so naive!

Three years into our adventure, our son was born. He was perfect in every way. Hubby and I were smitten and—we thought—prepared for our new role. Needless to say, we had A LOT to learn! Nearly three years later, our precious daughter entered the world, and our family was complete. After years of baseball (him), ballet (her), and battles (them!), our adult "children" are now charting their own courses. Sibling conflicts are the stuff of great stories between son and daughter, who are now the best of friends.

Today's 3-Word Wisdom—Celebrate Your Children. It sounds cliché, but kids really do grow up much too quickly. To those of you in the throes of child-rearing, savor the moments—even the messy, tearful, tantrum-filled ones. All too soon, you will be waxing nostalgic about those all-nighters spent walking your colicky baby. Mercifully, those memories will evoke the love you felt for that little bundle—and mellow the frustration that consumed you all those years ago. We will forever celebrate our children—our two most important accomplishments!

10. KEEP FAMILY CONNECTED

I was an "uh-oh" baby. My then 40-something parents had not intended to bring another child into the world—with a 14-year-old daughter and 19-year-old son, Mom and Dad had nurtured their young family through the Depression and World War II. They were beginning to see the light at the end of their childrearing tunnel. Then along came Paula, and their journey as parents continued.

Brother and Sister married early, and little Paula became Aunt Paula at the ripe old age of five. My first nieces and nephews were age-appropriate substitute siblings during my childhood. I would eventually be Aunt Paula to my brother's brood of three and my sister's gaggle of four. Sunday dinners, picnics at the park, and holiday gatherings kept us connected. Yet my late entry into the family left some of the family secrets off my radar—for many, many years. It would not be until my parents' and sister's death that the story would be retold...

Sister's firstborn was conceived when she was sixteen and unwed. The 1950s version of *16 and Pregnant* wasn't an exploitative TV reality show. Instead, it was masked in shame and secrecy. Frightened young girls were sent to "homes" to finish out their very visible months of childbearing, and their newborns were whisked from them upon delivery—into the arms of adoptive parents. One family's unbridled joy was another new mother's unimaginable sorrow and shame. I was a two-year-old toddler during this chapter of our family history. No photos or family letters in those boxes I mentioned earlier recount the tale. My brother had been in the army and was kept minimally informed. That was how it was done back then.

My sister eventually married the father of her firstborn. Together they had four more children and lost another, born prematurely. Divorce ended their marriage, and my sister struggled to support her children. A tragic accident took her son when he was in his 30s, and cancer eventually claimed my sister's life when she was 58. Hers was never an easy journey, but through it all she loved her children unconditionally, and she silently suffered her shame and sorrow about her first "lost" son.

It was during Sister's last year that she revealed his existence to her three daughters. Her searches for him had always led to dead ends. She had sketchy information at best, yet before she died, she wanted to meet the boy she had given up. Sadly, that did not happen—and her daughters promised Sister on her deathbed they would continue the search. They had another full biological brother out there—somewhere. And like their mother's, their efforts to find him were futile.

Sister is sorely missed by us all—especially by her girls, who keep their mother's memory alive for their children with photos and stories of Grandma. She had been gone eight years when, on a summer night in 2003, one of her daughters got the call. A woman was calling on behalf of her husband. She politely asked a couple of questions—"Was your mother's name ___? Was your father ___?" In that instant, my niece knew. "Are you calling about my brother?" She was! His wife made the call that changed their lives forever. He had found his family in less than three days of investigating. Needless to say, the tears flowed, and we joyously welcomed Sister's firstborn into our—and now his—family.

Today's 3-Word Wisdom - Keep Family Connected. A week later I hosted a "Meet Your Family" reunion to introduce my nephew to his new-found "clan". He lived a short 15 miles from us all those years. Whenever I am with her family, I can feel Sister there, too—at peace, with her other two heavenly sons—sharing the joy of wonderful family moments. Keeping us connected.

11. Learn
Something New

Is technology getting more complicated, or am I losing brain cells at a rate faster than you can program your DVR with a universal remote? I like to think that I am pretty tech-savvy "for my age." My current workaday world is dependent on my ability to navigate a complex customer relations management database, log into any number of conference lines, and access and analyze the myriad of data to create a meaningful report. When this technology fails me, I do my very best to sound intelligent with the IT support specialist at the other end of my phone call. "Don't sound like a tech-illiterate," I hear myself thinking. "That's a dead giveaway that you're an old fart." I can proudly say I have held my own in most of these encounters. Yet ask me to configure our TV to record two programs while I simultaneously watch Netflix, and all bets are off. Is there a *Baby Boomer's Guide to Technology* out there? If so, it will be on my birthday wish list! I am determined to keep up with technology—and I'm an advocate for lifelong learning of any kind.

One of these days I will retire, and I am looking forward to my post-60 education. The curriculum will be of my choosing, and the only prerequisite will be my interest in the subject matter. Here is my tentative class schedule:

- Advanced bread baking. Artisan breads, rolls, and baguettes. Imagine the aroma of the homework!
- French Pastries 101. Croissants, tarts, napoleons—got butter?
- Photography for the camera-challenged. Also known as remedial photography, this course will "focus" on keeping one's thumb away from the lens, removing the lens cap before looking through the thing you look through, and positioning subjects to avoid the appearance of a tree growing out of their heads.
- Photoshop for the camera-challenged. Taught in conjunction with the photography class above, students will learn how to remove tree trunks from the tops of subjects' heads.
- Motor home driving lessons. Hubby may veto this class, but I am determined to take a cross-country road trip. Would he prefer we sleep in the back of our SUV?
- Falling as an art form. This will be a required course, since I am a true klutz. Students will learn 1) to pay attention to their surroundings, and 2) how to fall with grace and style. A failing grade will require the purchase of an "I've fallen and I can't get up" necklace.

Today's 3-Word Wisdom—Learn Something New. Find opportunities to explore your hidden talents, and make the time to develop them. Keep your brain cells active and be open to change—it will happen.

Now, pass me the remote—and a croissant.

12. YOU ARE BEAUTIFUL

A friend recently shared an experience… A Post-it note, randomly affixed to a box of pasta at a local market, caught her eye in its unlikely placement. Curious, she stopped to read the handwritten message. It said, *"You look GREAT today!"* along with a website URL, operationbeautiful.com. Her experience compelled me to visit the website and read their mission:

"The goal of the Operation Beautiful website is to end negative self-talk or 'Fat Talk.' If this little blog only does one productive thing, I hope it helps readers realize how truly toxic negative self-talk is—it hurts you emotionally, spiritually, and physically."

How do they accomplish their mission? The simple answer is in their slogan:

"Transforming the way you see yourself, one Post-it at a time." How powerful. Sign me up!

I have struggled with weight and body image issues since early childhood. After my customary baby boomer tonsillectomy, sickly little Paula's health gradually improved—as did my appetite! By age 10, I was "pleasantly plump," my weight-obsessed aunts would tell me.

I vividly recall the first sting of pain and humiliation I felt when a boy called me "fatty" in front of our entire fifth-grade class.

I dealt with the pain by eating—and keeping to myself—which thereby perpetuated my feeling of self-loathing. I cringed with embarrassment when my mom took me school shopping in the boldly marked "Chubby Girls" section—a moniker I despised—at the Lane Bryant clothing store. I was mortified—and fearful that someone who knew me might walk past the store and see me in the fat girls' department. That label haunted me as a child. I spent my junior high and early high school years in the company of the small group of classmates who accepted me in all of my pudgy glory. Age, activity, and my first self-imposed diet (Instant Breakfast and Metrecal) eventually whittled off the extra pounds. By my senior year, I was at a socially acceptable weight, but I continued to see myself through that "fat lens" into adulthood.

All these years later, I still deal with weight and self-image issues. For years I yo-yo dieted, and in my 30s I reduced myself into early-onset menopause and near anorexia—yet I never saw myself as thin enough. Thankfully, Hubby did. He has always been my very own "operation beautiful" advocate and has helped me overcome the occasional negativity that still creeps into my conversations with myself. I have a much healthier relationship with food now. Yet the memory of those hurtful comments and the subsequent negative body image issues still linger. It is an ongoing struggle—yet one that I am committed to overcoming. Tomorrow I'm getting a supply of pretty Post-its to start spreading the Operation Beautiful love—and maybe attaching a couple on my own mirror!

Today's 3-Word Wisdom—You Are Beautiful. You are perfect just the way you are. Love your lines, your hips, your breasts, your belly. Love yourself. Focus on healthy habits and devote your life to being happy in your own skin.

You look GREAT today!

13. PARENT WITH PATIENCE

We have two wonderful children. Son and Daughter live nearby, and we see each other regularly. Son is engaged to a beautiful young woman, and Daughter is in a relationship with a charming young man. Hubby and I are so proud of the adults they have become!

As new parents, we mapped out a well-charted course for our children's upbringing. We were well-read on the subject of childrearing, and we were naive enough to believe our knowledge and nurturing would lead to a conflict-free parent/child dynamic. It was going to be easy, we were prepared—and we would show everyone how to be model parents. Ha!

Okay, you can stop laughing. As most of you know, nothing can truly prepare you for parenting—and as important as nurturing is, the undeniable variable in the equation is Nature! Children come pre-wired. As parents, you must understand how your child is genetically programmed and adjust your parenting accordingly.

Son was a fearless thrill-seeker. No fence was too high, no water too deep. An unattended moment in the backyard resulted in him scaling the fence to climb onto the roof—at four years old! Daughter, on the other hand, once stood outside—pitifully drenched by a sudden cloudburst—and would not cross our quiet cul-de-sac street alone until we waded through the puddles to hold her hand. Two kids. Same parents. Identical parenting philosophies—and exasperatingly different wiring! To say raising children is a challenge is an understatement. To those fortunate few with the enviable combination of childrearing expertise and "easy" kids, this point may be lost on you.

My 3-Word Wisdom—Parent With Patience. Your role as mother or father will test your will. Accept that fact and be willing to deal with the unexpected. Parenting is your biggest responsibility, and the adults your children become will be your reward for your perseverance—that, and their gift of grandchildren!

14. WEAR FABULOUS FOOTWEAR

It's time for some silly wisdom, and a confession. I love shoes. Not the *Sex and the City* variety, Jimmy Choos—too pricey! I'm a Designer Shoe Warehouse kind of gal. Hubby doesn't get it. Why on earth would one person need so many pairs? It's simple, really. Shoes fit—even when my skinny jeans don't. And while they don't always make my feet happy, the perfect heels matched with the right dress make any temporary foot discomfort bearable. Any shoe worshiper understands this love-hate relationship. Everyone else may as well stop reading farther.

Hubby has called me Imelda for years—a reference to the former Philippines' First Lady, Imelda Marcos, whose 3,000 pairs of footwear are worthy of a museum! While my collection is nowhere near Imelda's, I must confess I can't travel without a variety of footwear for every conceivable activity and outing. Hubby, however, packs the simple trinity—tennis shoes/sandals/ golf shoes. His closet shoe racks easily contain his brown-and-black/dress-and-casual collection. My shoe wardrobe runneth over, even though I have pledged to say good-bye to one old pair for every new addition to the collection. My dilemma lately has been my lack of opportunity to don an adorable mule or strappy sandal—I work from home in my sweats!

In super adulthood, the conventional wisdom of footwear is to be sensible—this is one rule I refuse to follow. I am going to make room in my closet for fabulous shoes of all colors and styles. Out with the business shoes, in with the party pumps!

Today's 3-Word Wisdom—Wear Fabulous Footwear. The shoes of my 60s are going to be sensational!

15. CALL YOUR MOTHER

As much as I loved both of my parents, my mother was probably the one person who made the biggest impact on my life. Her influence was not the result of an overbearing presence. There were no lectures. I don't remember a cross word or unkind comment. She was friendly, tolerant, and intelligent—and she had a wicked sense of humor. Mom's love was unconditional, and she and Dad always trusted me to make the right decision. As a teenager, my biggest deterrent to the temptation of breaking the rules was not the fear of making my parents mad—much worse was the thought of letting my parents down. As an adult, when faced with a difficult decision, I often asked myself, "What would Mom have done?"

Mom was considerably older than my friends' mothers, and I went through a period during my early childhood when I was ashamed of my parents' gray hair and seniority compared to my classmates' parents. Children can be cruel, and I was embarrassed when kids would call my parents old—or shopkeepers would address them as my grandparents. I adored Mother and Daddy, and I was conflicted about the love I felt for them and my secret desire for them to be younger. Thankfully this period was not long-lived, and some of the tales became the stuff of funny family lore in later years. Yet when I was a young adult, their advanced age had a more profound impact on me. I faced the reality of their mortality—and realized they would likely not live to see my young family grow.

I was in my early 30s when Mom died. I was not ready for her to go. We thought she was in the hospital to be healed, yet she never came home. I visited her on the day that was to be her last—yet I didn't know that the casual peck to her cheek was going to my final kiss good-bye. I had so much more to learn from her—so much to thank her for. The first few years she was gone were the most difficult, and more than once—when I had great news to share—my first instinct was to call Mom. Her absence from my life left a huge void. Mom has been gone for 26 years, and I still miss her. Yet she is always with me, as I continue to reflect upon her as my model of a truly beautiful person.

Today's 3-Word Wisdom—Call Your Mother. If you are fortunate to still have your mom in your life, make time to let her know you care. Savor the time you have with her, and show your appreciation for the lessons she has taught you. To my dear nieces and friends who also lost their mothers too soon, I can never replace her but will always be here to offer motherly advice.

That's what Mom would have done.

16. Save Stuff Wisely

In an earlier wisdom, I encouraged letter writing—and letter saving—as an invaluable and memorable source of family history. Now it's time to address the downside of my earlier wisdom. Mailing letters and keeping letters are two separate animals.

Let's just say I am a keeper. I am the family's designated keeper of stuff. I have drawers, chests, boxes, and closets full of stuff. I assure you, I am nowhere near needing the help given to TV's *Hoarders*, but I am guilty of hanging on to the flotsam and jetsam of life's special moments. One of my resolutions for this Big 6-0 year is to clear out some of the stuff—but it's not as simple as filling recycle bins and calling the Goodwill truck for a pick up.

The stuff I refer to goes beyond the letters—way, way beyond! Samples of my kids' school papers, projects, and progress reports since pre-school. College textbooks and binders of class notes Hubby and I can't seem to part with. Newspapers from any number of momentous, life-changing days in history. Boxes of photos and memorabilia my family has entrusted to me (actually, now that I think about it, I suspect they were simply getting rid of *their* stuff!). To some, it's history. To others, it's just clutter and closet filler. To me, it is all priceless. Yet when all is said and done, is it the stuff or the memories associated with the stuff I am hanging on to? If I let go of the tangibles, will those moments be lost?

The time has come for some tough "stuff" love—deciding what goes and what stays. My dilemma will be choosing what I unceremoniously relegate to the recycle and trash bins, and what will be passed on to the new stewards of the family history. It will be no easy task, and I suspect the "keep" pile will tower above the "send it on" and "toss it" stacks. If any of my scrapbooking relatives read this, consider this a pitiful cry for help!

Today's 3-Word Wisdom—Save Stuff Wisely. Treasure what's important—learn what to keep, what to share, and what to let go of. Savor life's events as precious memories. Be selective with the keepsakes and learn to keep only the truly significant memorabilia. Your family will thank you. Craigslist, here I come!

17. DO THE WORK

If life gave us do-overs, I would have continued my piano lessons—and my cello lessons—and my guitar lessons! I am a music lesson dropout. When I was a child, music practice was torture, and the beginner music selections were dreadful. I wanted to play the piano like my mother, who did not read music and simply kept a handwritten list of the song titles that were her repertoire. In her youth, Mom also played banjo in an all-girl band—the Merry Melody Maids. Besides the piano, she would occasionally pick up a banjo or ukulele and strum some fun little ditties. It evoked scenes right out of the movie *Some Like It Hot*! It was wonderful to hear Mom play. Music filled our house, and Sunday dinners with Brother, Sister, and their families were always punctuated with happy sing-alongs. I didn't have my mother's musical ear, so I was relegated to tedious scales and boring lesson book tunes. It didn't take long for the novelty to wear off, and piano lessons ended.

My next foray into music—a year and a half as a cellist—was not by choice. I had wanted to play the violin in our elementary school orchestra, but by the time they got to me, the only stringed instrument left in the music room closet was the cello. Mother assured me it was like the violin, just bigger! My sister had played the cello, after all—I had to continue the family's cello legacy. I remember lugging that clunky thing to and from school twice a week while my best friend easily toted her cute little violin case. Overweight Paula with her oversized violin! After one spring concert, I left the cello behind and had an instrument-free junior high school experience.

The folk music of the '60s inspired me to take one more stab at finding my inner musician—I got a guitar. No lessons required. No music to read. Simply follow the patterns in a chord book. How hard could it be? I strummed along to Peter, Paul, and Mary. I mastered the chords in Simon and Garfunkel's songbook. But strumming chords had limitations, and before long I lost interest in yet another instrument.

Two good friends did not give up on their love of music—these two guitarists have music coursing through their veins. One of them just returned from New Zealand, where he played to 15,000 fans—his guitar is his livelihood. I watch their fingers fly on acoustic and electric guitars, and I imagine myself making music of my own—if I had kept playing. For them, like my mom, the music comes from within—and with practice. I know I lack the innate talent of true musicians, but in my do-over scenario, I will power through the necessary basics in order to take my music to a new level. I think I'll find a new instrument to play into retirement!

Today's 3-Word Wisdom—Do the Work. If you really want to master something, take the time to lay the groundwork. As tedious as the preparation may be, your reward will be the sweet music of a job well done.

18. DANCE WITH ABANDON

One of the joys of writing has been the wonderful feedback I have received. Some of the most delightful comments have come from a high school acquaintance who, like me, is celebrating her Big 6-0 this month. She and I knew of each other in school, but she was among Hubby's group—cool kids—and I was on the periphery with my small circle of bookish, geeky misfits. Our paths rarely crossed, and we might have never met again but for the inception of social media. We are Facebook friends and are facing 60 together as if we are one! We live hundreds of miles apart and have not seen each other for over 40 years—yet she has extended a virtual hand and invited me to dance my way into the next decade.

I have always loved to dance. Not the ballet or tap lessons of my daughter's childhood. My earliest dance instruction came from then-teenage Sister. I was her dance partner as we watched Dick Clark's *American Bandstand* in the late '50s. I loved how she swung and twirled me to the innocent rock-and-roll tunes of the day. Mom and Dad did their part and taught me the Charleston and fox-trot—the dances of their youth. Our German friends introduced me to the polka, and my college roommate and I spent every Thursday night at the local Greek restaurant, assembling for whatever folk dance the instructor was offering that evening. Dancing has always made me happy—and Daughter, nieces, friends, and I have spent many a girls' trip on any number of dance floors, moving to the music. Thankfully no cameras have recorded us—I hope!

Hubby and I still love to dance. We have been partners for so long that we know the subtle hold or hand grip that signals the flow from one step to the next. It's not *Dancing with the Stars*, but it is ours. No one else exists when I am in Hubby's arms, and when the occasional onlooker stops by to tell us how cute we are, I'm never quite sure if it's meant as a compliment!

Today's 3-Word Wisdom—Dance with Abandon. Let go of your inhibitions and let the music you love inspire you. Grab a partner and dance in public—or dance alone in the privacy of your home. Feel the freedom of movement and forget your worries.

I promise you that whatever your mood, dancing will make you happy.

19. HAVE FRIENDS OVER

It's Saturday evening, and Hubby and I are home, alone. Daughter and boyfriend declined our invitation in favor of a dinner and movie date night. Son and fiancée also sent regrets and are home, enjoying their own quiet evening. Our sweet rescue golden retriever, Lucy, just ate the last of the grilled shrimp we had for dinner, and Hubby made a lovely fire to keep us warm as we await the arrival of a late winter storm. He's controlling the remote, and I am lingering over my laptop—searching for Wisdom. Tonight is a far cry from many weekend nights at our home…

Our house is get-together central. From carefully planned weddings and engagement parties to impromptu potlucks and pizza parties, we love hosting a houseful of friends and family. It's in our genes. I recall the gatherings my parents hosted—Fourth of July barbecues with barely legal fireworks, and the annual New Year's Day Rose Bowl game/chili fest with Dad's incomparable recipe. Hubby's parents also welcomed family for summer pool parties and Christmas Eve gatherings. During our parallel middle-class existence, growing up in the San Fernando Valley of the '60s, a night out was a night in—surrounded with the people you cared the most about, sharing food, stories, and inexpensive fun.

We had a lot of wonderful role models when it came to entertaining. Besides our parents, Brother and his wife were extraordinary hosts. Sister-in-law added delightful special touches to her events. Her attention to detail was not lost in me—she was my Martha Stewart! When the family gathering baton was eventually passed to me, I knew I had huge shoes to fill. The pressure was on, and I went to great lengths to ensure my events had the same impact on my guests as those gatherings of my childhood had on me.

I will admit my inner Martha finds personal satisfaction with my origami toilet paper folds (I am known for my extra rolls of TP, neatly displayed with a special fan-folded first sheet!). However, it took me several years to realize that great gatherings are measured by the enjoyment of the guests—not the matching plates and napkins, or crystal wine glasses. Our parties are memorable for the wonderful people they bring together—old and new friends, sharing food, music, and conversation.

Not everyone possesses the entertainment gene—or the backyard that will accommodate up to 100 guests! But I believe there is an innate human desire to spend time in the company of others. Sharing time at home with any number of special family and friends is one of our favorite pastimes and is, I hope, one of yours. Now get your party started—and be sure to invite us!

Today's 3-Word Wisdom—Have Friends Over. It can be simple or elaborate, large or intimate. The menu can be gourmet, potluck, or takeout. Bring the people you love together, and make no apologies for your home or your mismatched dishes. A night with loved ones at home is an unforgettable experience.

20. ACT YOUR AGE

Let's face it. We are a culture of age profilers. Society has carefully marketed a range of socially acceptable behavior and age stereotypes. As parents, we prepared ourselves for the terrible twos, the inquisitive threes, and the social fours. We have been programmed to assume teens are defiant and 20-somethings are adventurous. The social expectations of the 30s are marriage and families, and by 40, our course has been charted as we lay the groundwork to enjoy the good life in our 50s.

So what are the 60s supposed to look like? Advertisers portray the decade as an all-out assault on the aging process. We buy sensible shoes. We have stylish disposable undergarment options and stroll along beaches, remembering the good old days. Our silver hair and wise smiles represent our super adult status, and we receive kind and loving comments on how good we look—for our age—by our young friends. Well, advertisers, I am not drinking your Kool-Aid! If this is how I am supposed to act, then I am not playing. Yours is NOT my 60s!

This baby boomer and her friends are redefining the new and improved decade. Mine includes all of the things I have always loved—"Opera Nights" with Hubby (the details held in romantic, confidential silence), celebrations with family and friends, and girls' nights out dressed in strappy sandals and fun dresses. My 60s will focus on healthy living in order to keep playing—for as long as I want! I have accepted my age, but I refuse give in to the stereotype.

Today's 3-Word Wisdom—Act *Your* Age. Define each stage in your life by being true to yourself. Take responsibility for your actions and make good choices along your life's journey. And if you want to play, then play! Treasure your health and enjoy the life you want—not the life you are expected to live.

21. Fill Your Dash

Today's wisdom comes from an inspirational poem, "The Dash" by Linda Ellis. I was not familiar with the poem when I first saw the phrase on the shirts worn by a team of fellow walkers at one of the Susan G. Komen 3-Day breast cancer walks in which Hubby and I participate every year. Their shirts had the image of a beautiful young woman who had lost her battle with breast cancer. Her name, along with her birth and death years, indicated she was clearly gone too soon. The team's name was "Filling Our Dash." Their message? The dates representing the years you begin and end your earthly life are less significant than how you live the years within them—represented by the dash separating the two dates. It is how you fill your dash that defines the person you are.

Last April, a special friend lost her four-year-long battle with ovarian cancer. She had filled her dash raising two children who would become extraordinary adults. She welcomed her first grandchild the same year her cancer was diagnosed and filled her dash with precious granddaughter time. She and her husband filled the dash between her chemo rounds with cruises and trips to reunite with long-lost family. Witnessing her strength in the face of death was both heartbreaking and inspirational. She was powerless over the outcome of her journey, but she took control of what she could. She planned her funeral service to the last detail—including the musical selections, the Bible readings, and the guardian angel pins with a turquoise stone—symbolic of ovarian cancer awareness—everyone would receive. In her final weeks, she set in motion a complete kitchen remodel of her home, and while she did not live to see its completion, she attended to every last detail and finishing touch. To her, it needed to be done—she wanted her husband to have what he would need to be self-sufficient in her absence. She even instructed her daughter to make sure her hubby knew the importance of correctly outfitting her beautiful stainless steel and granite designer kitchen with the proper accessories. Norma, your kitchen is a masterpiece, and you are dearly missed—and you are my inspiration for filling one's dash.

Today's 3-Word Wisdom—Fill Your Dash. Life can be fleeting—don't take it for granted.

Live life to its fullest, make a difference, and consider the legacy of your life's "dash."

22. Conquer a Fear

In 2004, Hubby and I were selected to be contestants on the television show *The Amazing Race*—it was our fifteen milliseconds of fame. We had not auditioned. In fact, Hubby had never heard of the show. The casting director met us while we were participants in the Susan G. Komen 3-Day, a 60-mile fundraising walk. It was a chance encounter—we were fellow walkers and had enjoyed a couple of conversations together during our journey. Apparently she was desperate to cast one last couple for their upcoming season, and we must have fit the "cute older couple" profile. We were offered the chance to head out in about two weeks, on a whirlwind world adventure, and would be gone for about 40 days. Sadly, we had to decline the offer—Hubby had commitments that demanded his attention.

In watching the season's episodes of "our" race, I imagined myself meeting the challenges of each week's adventures. Would I have been able to rope a llama? Feed a lion? Could I have mustered the courage to zip-line across a gorge in the mountains of Peru?

Those of you who know me are already laughing. I am not a thrill-seeker. I avoid scary movies. During my skiing days, I was happiest on the beginner runs. When I travel, I am the one who actually checks the location of the nearest emergency exit row. Some would call me a fraidycat—I like to think of myself as sensible. Yet, as each stage of *The Amazing Race* challenged the contestants to some sort of physical or mental test, I found myself wanting to prove to myself I could overcome a fear and face a challenge.

My personal *Amazing Race* moment occurred a couple of years later. I had always been uncomfortable with heights and had a dreadful fear of falling (ask Hubby about our honeymoon, and my panic attack when I thought our elevator was plummeting from the 28th floor—it wasn't, by the way!). The episode that had contestants zip-lining across the Huambutio Gorge in Peru looked incredible. I wanted to do that, and my opportunity came while we were in Maui. Zip-line adventures were offered on the upcountry slopes of the Haleakala Crater. This was going to be my moment. Hubby and I signed the release, strapped on the harnesses and helmets, and hiked into the jungle—and then I leapt off a platform and let myself fly across the canyon to the other side—five different times! It was indescribable, and there was such sublime satisfaction in facing a formerly unthinkable challenge. The empowerment was one of my life's most liberating moments. I am still no thrill-seeker, but my zip-line experience taught me that I can do something outside my personal comfort zone and be a stronger person as a result.

Today's 3-Word Wisdom—Conquer a Fear. Staying within your perceived safety zone all the time limits your potential and cheats you out of opportunities that will enrich your life. Face your fear head-on and imagine the satisfaction of taking control. You can do it!

23. DITCH THE DOUBTERS

Yesterday on my morning walk, I let myself meet up with someone who I really don't like. It was Doubting Paula, and she was in my head—doing all she could to get my attention. She is not my friend. She is glass-half-empty Paula, and she is looking at 60 as an end, rather than a beginning. I have approached every other decade with optimism for what's in store—the start of a wonderful new chapter in life. But suddenly Doubting Paula reared her ugly head and did her best to sell me a different script—one in which I must say good-bye to my pre-60 self.

Doubting Paula tried to undo all of the positivity I have been focusing on these past weeks leading up to the Big 6-0 birthday. And what's worse, she made me cry. How dare she rain on my birthday parade?

I picked up my walking pace and left that bitch in the dust. Doubting Paula is a total downer. She fills my head with thoughts of what I have not accomplished. She sees almost-senior-citizen Paula, not super adult Paula who is going to rock her 60s with all she's got. I may even throw myself a party—and guess who's NOT getting an invitation!

Today's 3-Word Wisdom—Ditch the Doubters. Those people—including the ones residing within your head—who cast a gloomy shadow and project negativity along your path don't belong in your life. Surround yourself with those who fill you with hope, optimism, and love. Life is too special a gift. Surround yourself with those worthy of sharing it with you.

24. Adopt a Pet

Hubby and I are dog people. My wedding dowry was my dog, a yellow lab mix that I named Kitty. Hubby, Kitty, and I were a happy family of three, and when Son and Daughter came into the world, she was their attentive guardian and loyal playmate. Kitty went to dog heaven 12 years later, and it took only three weeks before we had another pet in our lives. Our golden retrievers Katie, Bear, Spencer, and Tracy eventually joined the family, and they shared all of our special moments over the years. As each one crossed the rainbow bridge, we tearfully said our good-byes, gently stroking our beloved "kids" as our vet administered the injection that would release them from their suffering. When our last golden, Tracy, left us, Hubby declared we would not get another pet—losing them was simply too difficult.

We would remain a pet-free family for five years...except for our neighbor's golden, Bogie, who became a daily visitor and helped us through our lost pet grieving process for those years. Last year Bogie's amazing 14-year journey ended—our neighbor came to our doorstep to tearfully deliver the news—and we suddenly felt the void of being completely without the company of man's best friend. It was time for me to confront Hubby's no-more-dogs mandate with an ultimatum of my own: we were going to get a pet—or else! Within days, our search began. We opted to rescue a golden retriever, and sweet Miss Lucy joined our happy family.

Lucy's backstory is not complete, but what we do know is that she was a puppy mill breeding machine who was dumped at the pound when her puppy-bearing years were over. She must have lived in a small kennel with no toys—only her puppies to mother—and no room to jump or play. She had to learn how to climb our stairs and has no jump instinct, likely due to her confinement in a cramped kennel for the first six years of her life. No amount of coaxing will entice her to hop up on the couch for a cuddle—and in hindsight this may be a blessing, considering her abundance of expendable fur! In her time with us, Lucy has slowly been discovering her "inner dog." She looks forward to her walks and has a basket full of soft plush toys—her "babies"—that she nuzzles and carries from room to room. She has discovered tennis balls but is not quite sure what to do with them once she captures them. Lucy is my constant companion, and as hard as it will be to lose her someday, Hubby and I know that in her time with us, we are giving her the life she has always deserved. We love Lucy!

Today's 3-Word Wisdom—Adopt a Pet. There are so many animals in need of a loving home, and while they may not be able to tell you in words, their soulful eyes will convey their gratitude for your kindness. There is no greater thank-you than the loving wag—or contented purr—of a rescued pet.

25. SHARE YOUR KNOWLEDGE

When our children were young, I did my best to provide thoughtful answers to their relentless questions. I was a teacher, after all, and I prided myself on having an explanation for every inquiry they threw my way. When Daughter questioned the spelling of her name—others with the same name used the customary spelling—I managed to convince her that hers was the phonetically correct version, and her like-named friends were the victims of an unfortunate misspelling. I loved the challenge of providing an answer to their queries, and in time I was regarded by the kids and their friends as the '80s and '90s equivalent of Wikipedia. Thankfully their questions were usually not math-related, and I was masterful at deflecting the unanswerable ones by redirecting them with a question of my own, "Why do *you* think the ocean water is blue in Hawaii and green in California?" I was good!

Of course, even the best and the brightest—and those of us who pretend we are—have a few gaps in our information cache. Occasionally I was at a loss to provide an acceptable response to one of Son's or Daughter's questions. I needed an escape clause, and I came up with the perfect disclaimer. I declared there were 17 things that I didn't know. From that point forward, when their questions had me stumped, the kids were delighted. "That's one of the 17 things!" they would exclaim. What followed were great moments of discovery as we shared the joy of learning something new—together. The kids relished the opportunity to uncover one of the 17 things, and with such a random number, I managed to retain my dignity—and my title as the uber-super-answer mom—long enough to survive the Childhood Inquisition. Of course, as they each reached the age of 17, Son and Daughter concluded that I actually knew nothing. I can now confirm that understanding the psyche of teenagers is definitely one of the 17 things I did not know!

My now-adult children still come to Hubby and me with questions—about life, love, and careers. They no longer need answers, but thankfully, they value our perspective. They are charting their own courses, and I cherish our conversations. If they ask me a question, I will share my knowledge and experience—but not necessarily an answer. That is now up to them.

Today's 3-Word Wisdom—Share Your Knowledge. Life is filled with teachable moments, and each of us is an educator. Cherish the inquisitive children in your life and help them discover the wonders of the world around them.

26. ENJOY THE DETOURS

This is it. I have officially proclaimed today as the beginning of my birthday week! I am putting on a cute new pair of boots, my skinny jeans, and a great top, and we are headed off to the wine country with friends to get my party started. If I had a birthday hat and noisemaker, I would announce to the world that this is Paula at 60! Let the fun begin!

I am in a much better frame of mind about this milestone than I was several months ago. I have to say the act of sharing some deeply personal stories and innermost feelings has helped me get in touch with super adult Paula—and guess what—I really like her! She is fun to be around. She is so appreciative of the love and support of her friends and family. She is proud of the life she has led and is determined to continue to make a difference in the world. She is dancing her way into the next decade. Super adult Paula is a really great broad!

Spending the past months reflecting on my life has been my prescription for dealing with some serious negativity that had invaded my usually upbeat nature. Writing required me to think hard about the person I am, the life I have led, and the path I want to take for the remainder of my days. My meltdown was a small bump in the road—and, if left unchecked, could have taken me dangerously off course—but I persevered. Now it's time to rock my 60s! I have so much to look forward to and will let all the young'uns know what the view is like from my new vantage point!

Today's 3-Word Wisdom—Enjoy the Detours. Don't let an unexpected change in course deter you from your final destination. As long as you know where you're headed, your inner compass will steer you in the right direction. Your detour may take you over some challenging mountains and unpaved roads, so let these be valuable lessons. You may be surprised by what you learn about yourself along the way.

27. Savor Life's Surprises

I am still in shock. Daughter, Son, family, and friends were gathering at our house yesterday while we took the aforementioned - and carefully plotted - diversionary trip to the wine country. As we made our way home and turned the corner onto our street, the sight was surreal—it took my breath away. There, lining both sides of our very long driveway, were over 100 people to welcome us. SURPRISE! Hubby and I arrived home from our fabulous wine-tasting day to a surprise 60th birthday party. A band played "Birthday" by the Beatles—our family's traditional birthday anthem. Caterers were cooking, and a bartender was pouring drinks. Banquet tables, chairs, balloons, banners, and canopy shelters—a last-minute necessity due to some uncooperative weather—filled the back yard. The home we had left in the morning had been transformed into a magnificent party venue, thanks to our wonderful children and the family and friends they enlisted to help.

Everyone asked, "Were you surprised?" Completely. Utterly. Totally. I did not want a party when Daughter asked about having some people over next weekend. We had plans for a future night out with the kids, and that sounded perfect. Besides, I felt that people were really over my Big Day after so much self-indulgent blogging. Little did I know what had been in the works for months!

I was stunned, as was Hubby, who was also kept completely in the dark. This was OUR 60th birthday party. We laughed and cried, hugged and danced—and apparently some unidentified neighbors called the police—at 8 p.m.—because we were making too much noise! It took 60 years to have someone call the cops on me—I am officially rowdy!

I am still trying to wrap my head around the entire night, letting it all sink in. Photos were being taken, and I am looking forward to reliving the night—it was all quite a blur! I want to say something profound to describe the sheer joy and gratitude I feel for the people who have filled my heart with love, but it will take some time to find the words. "Thank you" is not enough, but for now, it's all I've got! This is Paula—speechless.

Today's 3-Word Wisdom—Savor Life's Surprises. We spend the majority of our lives carefully planning and executing our days. If you are the recipient of an unexpected kindness—no matter how large or small—enjoy the surprise. And remember to say thank you—even when you are left speechless.

28. MAKE A DIFFERENCE

Ralph Waldo Emerson wrote: "The purpose of life is not to be happy. It is to be useful, to be honorable, to be compassionate, to have it make some difference that you have lived and lived well." In these words, I see the guiding truth that has had such an impact in my life. I am most satisfied when I am giving back. It took reaching my 50's to realize this, after making some career choices that pitted financial security over personal satisfaction.

From an early age I knew I wanted to be a teacher. My slightly younger and ever-present nieces and nephews, along with the neighborhood gaggle of kids, were the first students at ten year old Paula's Summer School – crafts, games, popcorn and Kool-Aid – two hours or so of distraction for the bargain rate of five cents a week! Even at a young age I knew teaching was a calling, and not a path to wealth! I loved my back yard teachable moments, and followed that passion to a teaching credential and my first career.

My years as an educator morphed into a variety of positions, teaching both gifted and learning challenged students, and eventually I was elevated to a position that took me out of the classroom and into the school district office. I loved my work, but being out of the direct daily contact of children left a void. I could not verbalize it, but I could feel it. I was missing the interactions that rewarded me with the satisfaction of having made a difference.

With Hubby's support, I took a huge leap of faith and followed my heart to open an educational toy and teaching supplies store. Bright Ideas was born and once again I felt inner satisfaction. I shared my expertise with the next generation of teachers eager to inspire their students. I comforted parents, worried their children were struggling with their studies, and assured them kids learn at a variety of speeds. I promoted learning as s fun adventure, and provided children the option of toys with purpose. Some of my best career memories had Bright Ideas as the backdrop.

Between Bright Ideas and my final work chapter, I had an opportunity to make a fresh new start with an entry level position in a very foreign (to me) and very large corporate setting. The thought intrigued me, and the prospect of advancement and future financial success was enticing. I was in my fifties and this late-in-life career change was based merely on stock options and 401k contributions. I was making the best choice based on money – not on my core beliefs. And I was a dismal failure.

Thankfully, I landed in the best of all possible places, and I now work daily with people dedicated to do whatever they can in the fight against breast cancer. My daily interactions are with cancer patients, survivors, or family members who have lost loved ones to this hideous disease. We laugh and cry together, and at the end of each day I have the immense satisfaction of knowing I provided them what they needed, with compassion and respect.

Today's 3-Word Wisdom—Make a Difference. Find your cause, identify your passion, and start today. Offer something of yourself that will make the world a better place. It is the greatest gift you have to offer—and the satisfaction is immeasurable. How are you making a difference?

29. SEEK YOUR WISDOM

With just two entries left to complete my "30 Toward 60" challenge, I am sad to be saying good-bye to the daily writing engagements with my laptop. When I began my "3-Word Wisdom" therapy, I had no idea where it would take me—I was behind the wheel with no GPS directing me. I allowed myself to think (a lot!) about my life. In reading my memoirs, I have confirmed what, in my heart, I already knew:

- I cherish my family and friends
- I need to love myself for who I am
- Each experience of my life—even the difficult ones—has contributed to the person I am
- I am happiest when giving back

Writing has always helped me deal with my innermost feelings, and sharing my thoughts and experiences with others helped me wrap my head around my birthday milestone and all of the anxiety I had allowed myself to feel. My 3-Word Wisdom project was my way of pushing myself to look inward on a daily basis, and as it wraps up, I feel a wonderful sense of accomplishment. I have tackled some very personal subject matter and shared a few never-before-told stories, and it has been liberating to "write out loud." My wisdom is just that—mine. Sharing it with you has been my personal journey of discovery. This has been Paula—unplugged!

Today's 3-Word Wisdom—Seek Your Wisdom. Each of

us has a lifetime of experiences—good, bad, and sometimes painful. Take time to reflect on your life, and ask yourself how your journey has been shaped by the choices you have made and the people you have encountered. Let your self-discovery provide enlightenment into the person you are, and be honest with yourself—are you the person you want to be? By getting in touch with your personal wisdom, you will have an inner compass to help you through life's best—and worst—moments. Here's to your best life. I already have mine.

30. LIVE EVERY DECADE

I made it! I am 60 today—and guess what? It didn't hurt a bit. I allowed myself to fret over this birthday—60 happens, folks—and putting my feelings into words helped me understand myself better. I am powerless over the number, yet I am in control of the contents of my life. I am determined to make my 60s the best they can be.

How am I celebrating the actual date of my birth? I'm going to Disneyland! Hubby and I had our second official date there back in 1971, and we still feel like kids in love at the happiest place on earth. For those who think it is utter foolishness for a pair of 60-year-olds to traipse—sans children—around a theme park, let me offer my "Disneyland Metaphor for Life." Strap on your mouse ears, and let's take a decade-by-decade tour of the Magic Kingdom…

Fantasyland is our magical childhood, when we "believe" with innocent, wide-eyed wonderment. We are dragon slayers and princesses (Hubby may argue that I still am!), and imagine flying like Peter Pan—protected from the scariest of villains by our corps of valiant heroes—and we find pure glee in the spin of a teacup!

Tomorrowland represents our turbulent teens, when we look forward to our birthdays—not for the year they represent but for their marker toward what lies ahead…our adulthood and freedom! We are thrill-seekers and dreamers—in a constant state of flux, like the dips and curves of Space Mountain. We drive the Autopia cars and imagine ourselves behind the wheel of our first set of wheels. During these years, we question if tomorrow will ever come.

Welcome to Adventureland and our 20s. The world is our playground. We are choosing our own adventure—making our own decisions—beginning to take college and work seriously and realizing the years of contemplating "What will I be when I grow up?" now require a decision! Lifelong friendships and relationships are made, and we entertain thoughts of starting our own families. Our Jungle Cruise 20s offer lots of humor, a few waterfalls, and a wild night—or two!

Our 30s mark our visit to Frontierland—and for many, the new frontier of raising children. Parenthood is life's most important career. I am astonished that, as much as we prepare for every other aspect of adulthood, we enter our child-rearing days with very little knowledge on the subject. Kids don't come with an instruction book—simply pre-charged batteries that never run out of energy. We are Davy Crockett charting a completely new territory, and our muskets and coonskin caps have been traded in for binkies and baby strollers.

We spend our 40s in New Orleans Square. The kids have taken over our home, and the pantry has been pillaged—we are living with the Pirates of the Caribbean! We have morphed into our parents, and the kids are sure we have no clue what it is like to be a teenager! We now worry about their curfews, and we are careful not to let them know what we did in our youth because, God forbid, they may figure out we were young once! We may need a cocktail now and then to survive their tests of independence—drink up, me hearties, yo-ho!

It's time to enjoy our satisfied 50s on good old Main Street—the kids are grown, our nest is empty, and we find ourselves waxing nostalgic. We are once again in the favor of our children who actually ask for our advice! Life is filled with great memories of days gone by. Thankfully our minds mask all of the child-rearing drama beneath a lovely veil—even the trying moments are magically transformed into treasured memories.

Where will our 60s take us? I am looking forward to finding out! Hubby and I will ring in our next decade by reconnecting with our inner children—recalling visits with our nieces, nephews, and children. Like Peter Pan, there is a part of us that never wants to grow up. We will immerse ourselves in unadulterated fun—and return tomorrow to reality and all that truly matters—with our unwavering commitment to making the world a better place.

Today's 3-Word Wisdom—Live Every Decade. Life is a wonderful adventure. Those of us of a "certain age" will recall Disneyland's ticket books, lettered A to E – the E ticket reserved for the most thrilling attractions. Enjoy your E-Ticket ride through life, filled with exciting—and unexpected—twists and turns. Allow yourself to experience all that life has to offer.

NEVER SAY NEVER

Fast-forward five years. Son and Daughter found and married their soulmates and gave Hubby and me the gift of two beautiful grandsons. We said tearful good-byes to friends, gone too soon, and I faced the fact I am now the only survivor of my nuclear family as I celebrated the life—and mourned the loss—of my brother. Hubby and I are as happy as ever, and actually healthier than we were at 60. 2016 marks our 42nd wedding anniversary, and retirement is on the horizon. We are still two kids in love!

After writing my 3-Word Wisdom posts for my blog, I was encouraged by my followers to write a book. I will admit that I was proud of the word count I had accumulated, but publishing a book? In true Paula fashion, I made every excuse why that would be impossible. I need a publisher. I've never taken a writing class. No one would be interested in reading what I have to say. The "can't" list was endless, and the pages and the blog lay dormant for five long years.

Hubby never stopped believing in me and would occasionally bring up the topic. When a new client of his—a successful self-published writer—shared her journey to authoring her first novel, Hubby conveniently found an opportunity to introduce us. That meeting left me educated, inspired, and motivated. Her advice was invaluable: "You already have a book. Stop overthinking it and publish it. Don't try to be perfect." Her mentoring, along with Hubby's patience and encouragement, have given me the inner strength I needed to cast my fate to the wind and set sail for this voyage. Destination? My first book.

My closing 3-Word Wisdom—Never Say Never. Allow yourself time to change. Let go of the fear of failure. Your time will come when you open your heart and mind to the possibilities.

Thank you all for taking this ride with me. You have made my journey to 60 a treasured gift, and I am forever grateful for having you in my life. I survived the '60s of my youth—here's to living my 60s of super adulthood!

With sincere gratitude,
Paula